Visual Thinking Puzzles

Michael A. DiSpezio
*Illustrated by **Myron Miller***

Sterling Publishing Co., Inc.
New York

Library of Congress Cataloging-in-Publication Data

Dispezio, Michael A.
  Visual thinking puzzles / by Michael A. DiSpezio ; illustrated
by Myron Miller.
      p.   cm.
  Includes index.
  ISBN 0-8069-9975-6
  1. Puzzles. 2. Visual perception. I. Miller, Myron, 1948– .
II. Title.
GV1493.D559   1998
793.73—dc21   98–6166
                                                          CIP

      7 9 10 8

Published by Sterling Publishing Company, Inc.
387 Park Avenue South, New York, N.Y. 10016
© 1998 by Michael A. DiSpezio
Distributed in Canada by Sterling Publishing
c/o Canadian Manda Group, One Atlantic Avenue, Suite 105
Toronto, Ontario, Canada M6K 3E7
Distributed in Great Britain and Europe by Chrysalis Books
64 Brewery Road, London N7 9NT
Distributed in Australia by Capricorn Link (Australia) Pty. Ltd.
P.O. Box 704, Windsor, NSW 2756 Australia

Sterling ISBN 0-8069-9975-6

Contents

Acknowledgments

Without the encouragement, dedication, and hard work of many people, publications like this one wouldn't be possible. Although I am fortunate enough to have my name on the book, I'd like to recognize the opportunities, experiences, and unselfish sharing of Alan J. McCormack and Cheryl L. Mason, both professors at San Diego State University. In addition to being my good friends, these colleagues supervise Project VISTA, a wide-ranging endeavor that looks at improvement in science education by exploiting the visual and spatial domains of learning.

I'd also like to thank my Sterling "team" who has worked together on several of these puzzles books. They include my editor Hazel Chan and artist Myron Miller. I'd also like to recognize Sheila Barry, for her continual support, encouragement, and insight into the project's creation.

Introduction

Think of a cardboard box that contains your favorite pizza. What color is the box? Is anything printed on the box? Is the box fully closed? Can you see any oil stains on the cardboard? Can you sneak a peak at the pizza within?

Now, slowly open the box. What shape is the pizza? Are any slices missing? Does the pizza contain any extra toppings, such as pepperoni or sausage. Do any of the slices have anchovies? Is the pizza piping hot or has it cooled? Did someone already spread hot pepper or garlic over the cheese?

Your ability to visualize this pizza experience reflects the incredible power of your "mind's eye." Visual thinking is a powerful element that defines the way in which we process all sorts of information.

Visual thinking isn't stuck in the present. We can use it to reflect back into the past. For example, think of when you first saw this puzzle book displayed on the shelf of a bookstore. Was it on an upper or lower shelf? Was it standing alone or was it part of a stack? Now imagine when someone first placed this book on the shelf. Think back even further to when another person delivered a box of these books to the bookstore. Perhaps you might even be able to think back to what might have been going on when the author was writing this introduction. That's the power of visual reflection.

Visual thinking can just as easily jump into the future. Think of a domino balanced upright on a desktop. Now, in your mind's eye place five other dominos close to this one so that a row is formed. Now, push against the first domino until it falls over. What happens as it strikes the next domino? Do all the dominos fall? What happens when the final domino tumbles? Do any of them fall off the table? Again it's that power of visual thinking that allows you to "fast forward" into the future.

This book contains a collection of puzzles that have been developed, tweaked, and twisted into mind-bending challenges that are sure to test your visual thinking skills. Many of the puzzles are based upon traditional challenges that have been around for hundreds of years. Others are brand new. But instead of me telling you about these eye-brain busters, why not experience them yourself? Open your eyes and mind and have fun!

—Michael

THE PUZZLES

WRAP IT UP

You don't need a crystal ball to see into the future. All you need is your brain.

The shape below is formed from three smaller pieces. These pieces are connected by a tiny hinge at their point of attachment. Suppose you were able to rotate the pieces so that neighboring sides aligned flatly and squarely. Which one of the shapes below could this structure look like?

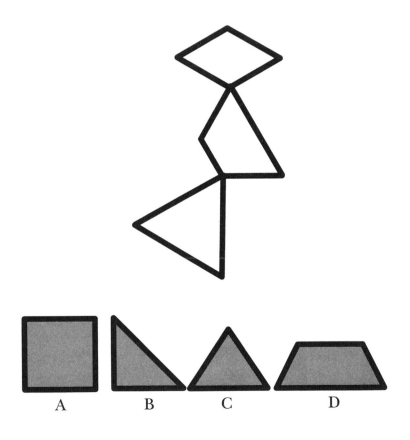

A   B   C   D

Answer on page 94.

PI PIECES

There are many skills we associate with visual thinking. Some of these skills may be much more difficult to master than others. For example, the ability to mentally rotate objects is often harder than we might imagine.

Try this: If you were to assemble these pieces into a circle, what would the figure formed by the inner lines look like?

Answer on page 81.

CONNECT THE DOTS

Here's a different type of puzzle. To solve it, your brain must uncover patterns.

How many squares can you create in this figure by connecting any four dots?

Note: The corners of the square must lie upon a grid dot.

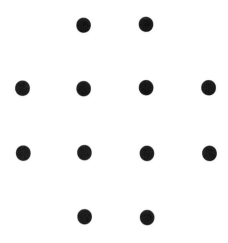

Answer on page 72.

PIZZA PI PROBLEM

Think about pizza. Imagine its sauce-and-cheese covered surface. Not too hard to do, is it? This ability to produce "images" within our brain is a product of visual thinking. Now, let's get back to pizza.

Bob likes to prepare personal pizzas. He begins with a circle of dough that is 12 inches in diameter. On top of the dough, he places slices of salami. All of the slices are round and have a 4-inch diameter. If Bob doesn't overlap the slices or allow any of the slices to extend beyond the edge of the pie, what is the maximum number of salami slices he can add?

Answer on page 82.

POINT THE WAY

There are all sorts of patterns. Here's one that is based upon a sequence in which some sort of change occurs over time.

Can you uncover how this sequence of tiles changes? If so, use what you've visualized to identify the fourth member of this series.

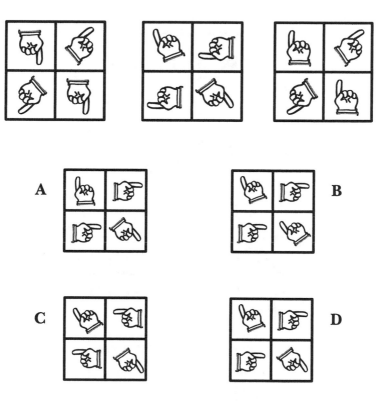

Answer on page 82.

MIRROR MADNESS

Do you realize that your brain is constantly trying to make sense of the information sent to it by your eyes? You may already know that the image that falls upon the retina of the eye is upside-down. Your brain, however, flips the image over into a more logical upright appearance. Perhaps your brain can flip images "on cue?"

"Mirror, mirror, on the wall, which of the choices below is the reflection of the following tile?"

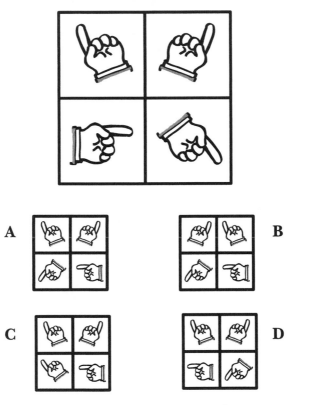

Answer on page 78.

SPACING OUT

For a moment, let's leave the eye-brain puzzles and just "space out."

A shuttle astronaut leaves her craft to work on a disabled satellite. She lands on one corner of the satellite (which is a perfect cube) and realizes that she must walk across the satellite's surface to the opposite corner. To conserve oxygen, she must follow the shortest possible route. Is her planned route (identified by the dotted line) the shortest path between opposite corners?

Answer on page 86.

CODE CAPER

What animal is represented in the code below?

Hint: From our earliest years, we learn to identify objects by the space they occupy. Artists, however, sometimes use the space that doesn't occupy something. It's called negative space and it's the fabric that surrounds things. Perhaps, a little negative space might help you solve this puzzle?

Answer on page 71.

LINK LATCH

Your optic nerve links the eye and the brain. This "connecting wire" is not passive. As messages travel along its path, visual information is analyzed and sorted. By the time they arrive at the brain, the messages have already been partially processed and analyzed so that no time is wasted.

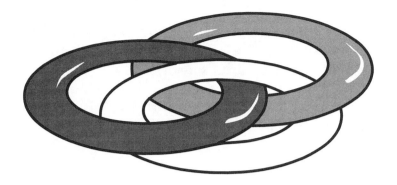

While digging through a box of links, a jeweler uncovers the three joined links shown above. She decides to separate the links. As she examines them, she finds a way to disconnect all three by opening just a single link. Can you?

Answer on page 78.

CUT THE CUBE

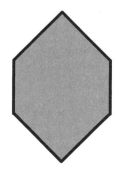

Can you visualize 3-D space? If so, imagine a solid block of clay shaped into a perfect cube. Can you visualize it? Great. Now, let's change it with a modeling knife. How can a single cut produce the six-sided face shown here?

Answer on page 94.

SQUARE DEAL

To solve this next puzzle, you'll need both visual thinking skills and a bit of eye-hand coordination (you'll also need a pair of scissors).

Trace the sections below onto a sheet of heavy-stock paper. Carefully cut them out with the scissors. Then arrange the pieces so they form a perfect square.

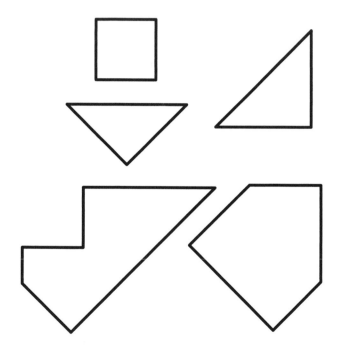

Answer on page 87.

REFLECTING BACK

Imagine the hands of a standard clock in the position that indicate the time of 4:20. Suppose you looked at that clock in a mirror. Which of the following clock faces would the reflected image resemble?

I II III IV

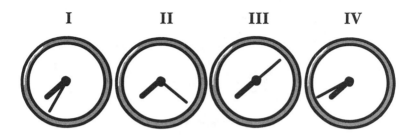

Okay, let's make it a bit more challenging. Suppose that the hands of a clock indicate the time of 2:40. Suppose you turned the clock upside down and then looked at its mirror reflection. Which one of the faces below would the reflected image resemble?

I II III IV

Answers on page 84.

NAUGHTY NOTES

And now a musical distraction... Which pair of notes is unlike the other six pairs?

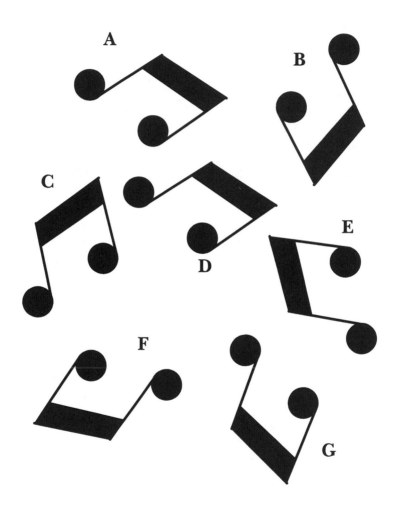

Answer on page 79.

AMAZE IN STRING

A pipe is located at the center of an odd loop of string.

Suppose the string is pulled by its two free ends. Will the string come free of the pipe or will it be caught by it?

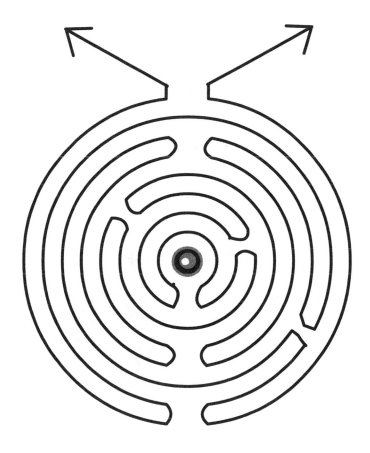

Answer on page 70.

BROKEN RECORD

A phonograph record falls to the floor and splits into two equal halves. Suppose that the halves are carefully glued back together so that all of the grooves align. There is, however, a slight problem. In the rush to repair the album, the incorrect sides are paired. Therefore, each side of the record is a composite formed by half of side A and half of side B. Now let's set this record on a turntable and place a phonograph needle at the end of the first song. As the record spins will the needle:

a) trace out a circle, always remaining the same distance from the center spindle?

b) spiral in towards the center spindle (its normal motion)?

c) spiral out towards the album edge?

Answers on page 70.

THIS SIDE UP

Make four copies of this arrow pattern. Cut out each arrow along its outline. Then arrange the copies so that they form five arrows.

Answer on page 90.

PREFAB 4

Suppose the following pattern was folded up or folded back to form a house. Which one of the structures below could *not* be formed from this pattern?

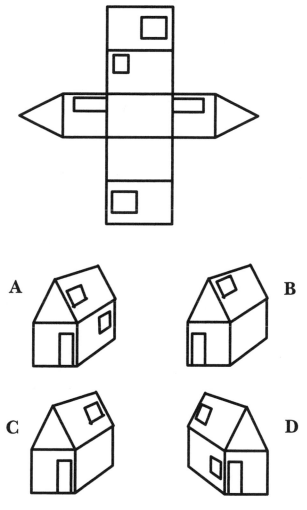

Answer on page 82.

SUPERIMPOSING POSITION

Suppose the values illustrated by the two graph forms below are added together. Which of the four choices will the combined final graph form look like?

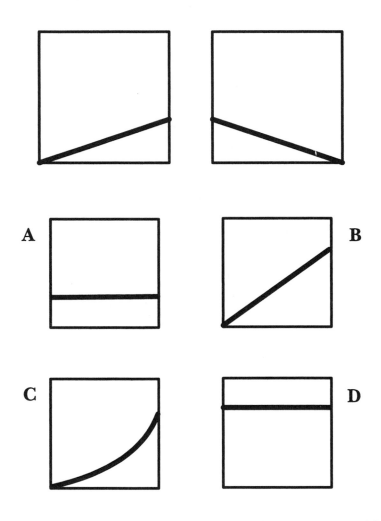

A

B

C

D

Answer on page 88.

HIDDEN IN PLANE SITE

Can you uncover fifteen squares outlined in the pattern below?

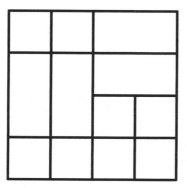

Answer on page 74.

WHAT SIGN ARE YOU?

The mathematical signs connecting the numbers below have been left out. Good thing we've supplied them on four tiles. Your job is to place the tiles between the numbers so that the final answer is 3. All operations are done in a left-to-right order.

Answer on page 94.

TYING THE KNOT

As these two lovers slurp up a shared piece of spaghetti, will a knot form in the pasta (or only in their hearts)?

Answer on page 92.

PENTAGON PIECES

Trace these two pairs of shapes onto a sheet of heavy-stock paper. Use a pair of scissors to carefully cut out all four pieces. Then rearrange the shapes into a regular pentagon.

Answer on page 81.

PENCIL STACK

Which is the third pencil up from the bottom of the stack?

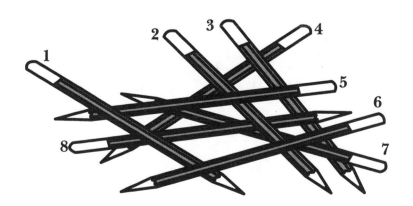

Answer on page 81.

BOXED IN

Which one of the following designs cannot be folded into a cube?

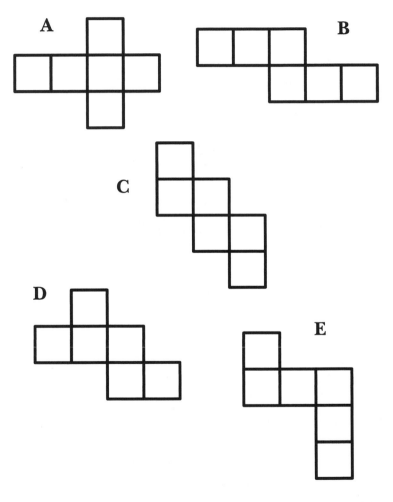

Answer on page 70.

FACES FRONT

Suppose you can examine this five-block shape (although hidden, the fifth block is present in the middle of the shape) from any angle. How many different cube faces can you count?

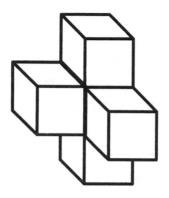

Suppose that hidden block (the fifth one) is evaporated. How many cube faces would now be exposed?

Now examine this nine-block shape from any angle. How many different cube faces can you count?

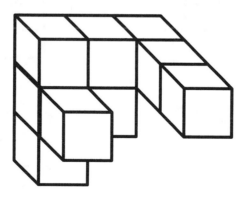

Answers on page 72.

IMPOSSIBLE PROFILE

Even though you can't see the entire block structure below, you can make accurate statements about its appearance. If viewed from all directions, which one of the four profiles is impossible?

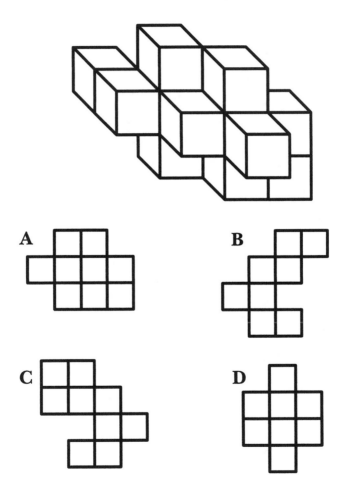

Answer on page 74.

PHARAOH FOLDS

Which of the folding patterns below will produce a shape unlike the others?

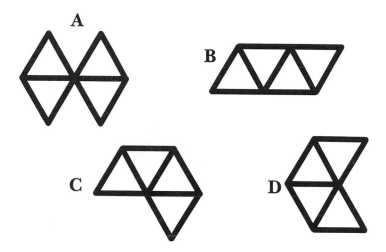

A

B

C

D

Answer on page 81.

BRAIN TRAINING

There are two parallel railroad tracks that connect the cities of Metropolis and Gotham City. Every hour, a train leaves from each city and travels to the other. The trip takes 3 hours in either direction. Suppose you are on board a train that is leaving Metropolis. Counting the inbound train that enters the Metropolis station as you pull out, what is the total number of inbound trains you will pass as you travel to Gotham City.

Answer on page 70.

HOW MANY TRIANGLES?

How many equilateral triangles can you uncover in the pattern below?

Answer on page 92.

ON THE MARCH

An army of neurotic ants lives in the jungle of some remote country. In their journey they've uncovered a trail formed by three overlapping circles.

Here's the challenge: The ants have to find a route that covers every part of this odd trail. The route can't cross over itself (nor can the ants back up and retrace any steps). Can you uncover their continuous route?

Here's route two with the same restrictions.

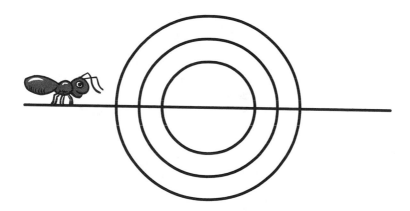

Answers on page 80.

STOP AND THINK

How many different paths can lead you through the octagonal maze below. From start to finish, you can only move in the direction of the arrows.

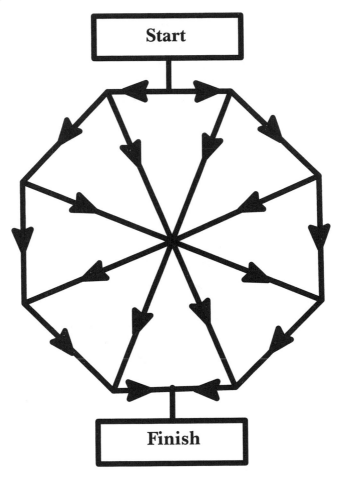

Hint: There is a way to do this puzzle without tracing out each path. Can you uncover the strategy?

Answer on page 88.

CIRCULAR CODE

What number belongs in the blank slice below?

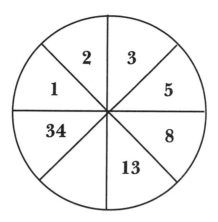

Answer on page 71.

SHAKES

Six people attended a gala for visual thinkers. If all guests shook hands with everyone else (no pair shook hands more than once), how many handshaking events were there?

Answer on page 84.

NESTING DOLLS

A nesting doll collected from the planet *Infinitum* contains a limitless number of smaller dolls. Each smaller doll is exactly half the size of the larger doll that it "nests" within. Suppose the outermost doll is one foot tall. If you are to remove all of the inner dolls (assume there are an infinite number) and place them on top of each other, how tall will the stack rise?

Answer on page 79.

THE WHOLE TRUTH

When John P. Cubic was placed on the stand, he was questioned about his puzzle-solving capability. He assured everyone that he was skilled in puzzeology.

To prove this, he displayed a cardboard square with an off-center hole. "By cutting this cardboard into two and only two pieces (and rearranging those pieces), I can move the hole into the center of this square." Although the jury was out, the lie detector supported his claim.

Can you figure out his cutting pattern?

Answer on page 90.

BLOCK HEADS

Which pattern of blocks is unlike the others?

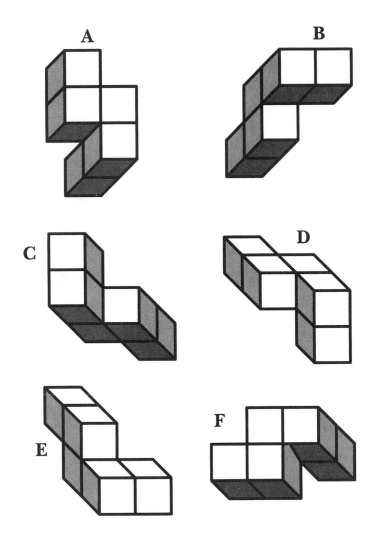

Answer on page 70.

FILL 'ER UP

Can you fill out the grid below using the following clues?

a) B is in the same column as E and H.
b) F is to the left of B and directly above D.
c) G is to the right of E and directly above I.
d) D is directly left of H and in the same column as A.

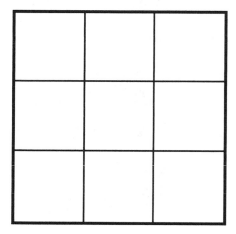

Answer on page 73.

The JIG'S UP

A jigsaw puzzle contains fifty pieces. If joining any two pieces (or groups of pieces) is considered one move, what is the fewest number of moves required to join all fifty pieces?

Answer on page 89.

THIS WHEEL'S ON FIRE

Examine the two sets of wheels below. The shaft that connects both sets of wheels is made of solid steel. In the top set, the shaft is attached at the same distance above each of the wheels. In the lower pair, the shaft is attached more towards the edge of the larger wheel.

If the small wheel spins in a clockwise direction, what will happen to the larger wheel? Will the motion of the larger wheel be different in the lower pair? If so, how?

Answer on page 93.

SQUARE GEARS

Suppose you were able to turn the top square gear. How much of a turn (if any) would the lower square gear make?

Answer on page 88.

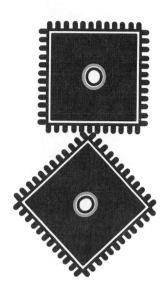

TOOTHPICK TRICKS

Arrange twenty-four toothpicks in the pattern below. Can you remove eight picks from this pattern so that only two squares are formed by the remaining picks?

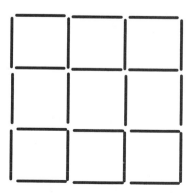

Arrange sixteen toothpicks in the pattern below. Can you *move* (don't remove) three toothpicks so that four squares of the same size are produced?

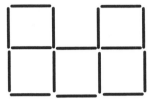

Build the house below using eleven toothpicks. Can you change the position of one toothpick to make the house face in the other direction?

Finally, arrange six toothpicks to make eight different triangles.

Hint: The triangles will be of two different sizes.

Answers on pages 90–91.

GOING TO PIECES

The below puzzle is entitled "White Cat on a Snowy Day in the Arctic." Suppose you have to completely color each piece so that no two adjoining pieces are the same color.

What is the minimum number of colors you need to distinguish each piece?

Answer on page 74.

PUZZLING PAGES

A blast of wind has separated the pages of a local newspaper. From the page numbers shown below, can you determine how many pages were in the complete newspaper?

Answer on page 83.

CONTROVERSIAL CUBE

Which two cubes below can be constructed by folding this pattern? Let's assume that the pattern is the "outside" of the material.

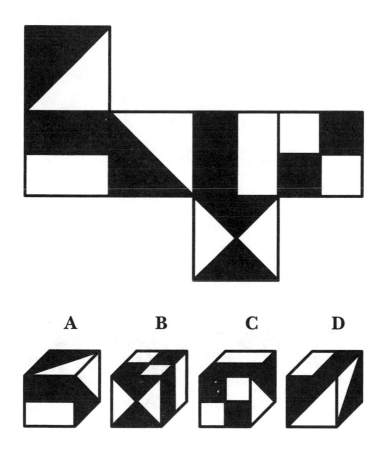

A   B   C   D

Answer on page 72.

FROM WHENCE IT CAME?

Now let's reverse the thinking process. Can you identify the outer pattern from which the cube was folded?

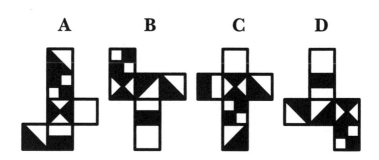

Answer on page 73.

SINK YOUR TEETH

Both cog A and cog D have sixty teeth. Cog B has thirty teeth. Cog C has ten teeth. Suppose cog B makes twenty complete turns every minute. Which will spin faster, cog A or cog D?

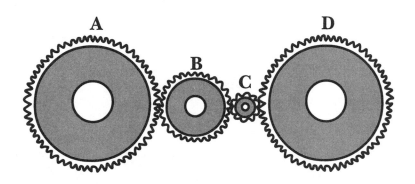

Answer on page 84.

HANDS-ON/MINDS-OFF

Examine each of these hands carefully. Then decide which one of the nine is unlike all the others?

Answer on page 74.

GOING IN CIRCLES?

Are the belts and wheels arranged so that they will spin freely as this mouse races up the treadmill?

Answer on page 74.

SPOTTY ANSWERS

Can you draw an equilateral triangle so that the three dots below are positioned on different sides of the triangle?

Let's add a side to the challenge. Can you draw a square so that each of the four dots below are positioned on different sides of the square?

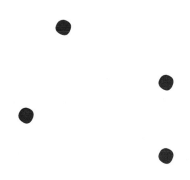

Answers on pages 86–87.

MORE SPOTS

Using only six straight lines, connect all of the sixteen dots shown below.

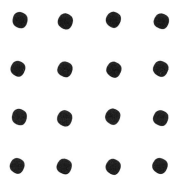

Answer on page 79.

CAFFEINE BREAK

The owners of a local coffee store ordered two different sizes of coffee pots. If pot A holds about 8 ounces of java, about how many ounces does pot B hold?

Answer on page 71.

SECTOR SEVER

Four alien civilizations are dividing up the universe. They encounter a sector of space that has this unique arrangement of planets. If all four civilizations are to get identical sectors of space (each containing three different planets), show how this region should be divided.

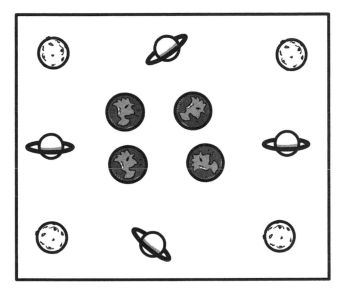

Answer on page 85.

MORE OF THE GREAT DIVIDE

The star map below gives the location of eleven stars. Can you give each star its own space by dividing the square with only five straight lines? The spaces don't have to be equal.

Answer on page 78.

LET THE GAMES BEGIN

When those aliens aren't dividing up the universe, they're engaging in competitive sports. So far, their favorite game is tug-of-war. During the competitions, there were three ties, which are illustrated below. From this information, can you determine which of the choices can balance the unfinished match?

A   B   C

Answer on page 76.

SNEAKY

Suppose you are able to crawl inside this sneaker that belongs to one of those alien athletes. Assuming that the laces always cross, what would the inner criss-crossed view look like?

Answer on page 85.

FOILING FOLDS

Suppose a square sheet of paper is folded and creased. Then a single snip of the scissors removes a corner of the fold as shown in the last step below. If the pattern is then unfolded, which square will it now resemble?

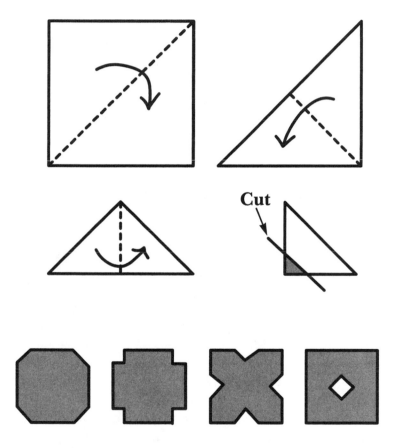

Answer on page 73.

SPIRAL BOUND

An astronomer photographs two side-by-side spiral galaxies. When she examines her files, however, she uncovers that one of the photos is of a different galaxy pair. Examine the six images below. One pair of spirals is unlike the others. Can you identify the different image?

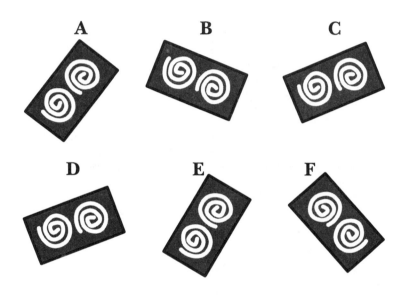

Answer on page 86.

IMAGINING DIGITS

In the numbers 1 through 100, which digit appears the most? While you're at it, in that same set of numbers, which digit appears the least?

Answer on page 74.

ROLL WITH IT

If you rolled this pattern into a cylinder, which one of the choices below will it look like?

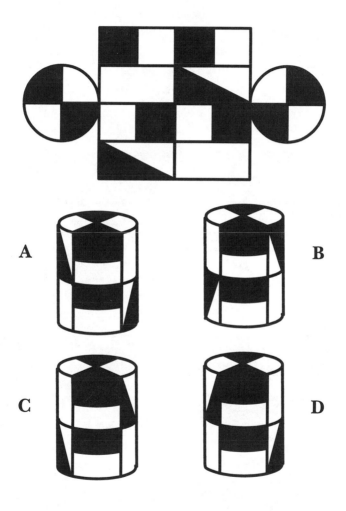

Answer on page 84.

OUT OF THIS WORLD
CONSTRUCTION

Orbiting above the earth are the four cubic sections of a soon-to-be constructed space station. Astronauts will assemble the four separate cubes into a four-cube station. The only problem is that the astronauts left the construction plans back on Earth. It's your job to determine how many different four-cube arrangements are possible. (The cubes can only be joined squarely and face-to-face.)

Answer on page 80.

INTO THE POOL?

Seven pool balls are placed in a pattern shown below. Can you rearrange the balls so that the sum of any three-ball line is equal to twelve?

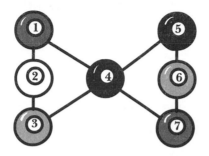

Answer on page 76.

SURE SHOT

Suppose the billiard ball strikes the bumper at the point identified by the arrow. If the ball has the energy to keep rolling, which pocket will it eventually sink into?

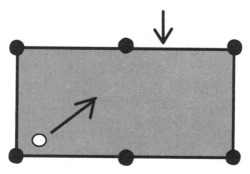

Answer on page 89.

COASTER CUT

Alas, the party is over and the amusement park is closed. The roller coaster ride has been sold. All that is left is this one section of track and frame. In order to be moved, the pattern must be divided into two identical parts. Can you do it?

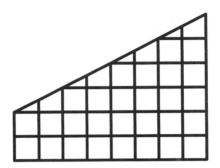

Answer on page 71.

SIZING UP SQUARES

How many different sizes of square can be made by connecting the dots that form this grid? And while you are at it, what is the total number of squares that can be created by connecting the pattern dots?

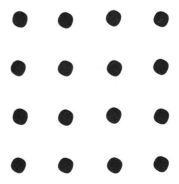

Answer on page 85.

THE CIRCLE GAME

Can you uncover the pattern in the following figure? If so, use what you've discovered to identify the number that should be placed in the center of the figure.

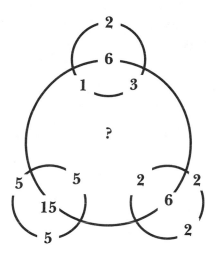

Answer on page 89.

WHAT'S NEXT?

Complete this sequence.

Answer on page 93.

VERY WELL VENN

A Venn diagram is a way of communicating relationships. For example, the following Venn diagrams show that 1) all beetles and all flies are insects and 2) some mammals and some insects can fly.

Using this type of visual scheme, sketch out Venn diagrams that illustrate the following:

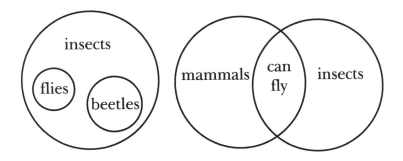

1. All ice creams are dairy products and all dairy products are food.

2. Some rockets use liquid fuel, some rockets use solid fuel, and the space shuttle uses both liquid and solid fuel.

3. All whales and all dogs have hair. All snakes do not have hair.

Answer on page 92.

RACK EM...AGAIN, AGAIN, AND AGAIN

The pool balls below are positioned in a six-ball rack. If you add the values of any three-ball edge, you'll come up with ten. Can you rearrange the balls within this rack to produce three other patterns that also produce equal-sum sides?

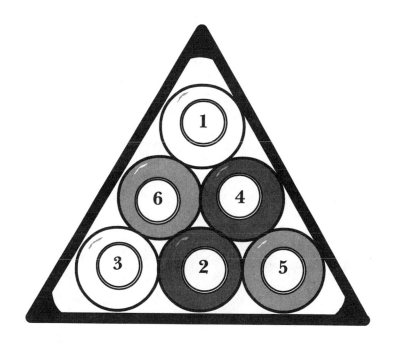

Answer on page 83.

DIAL DILEMMA

The instruments in a cockpit are positioned so that a pilot can quickly glance at the indicators and know instantly if there is a problem. In the panel below, one dial does not fit the pattern. Can you locate it quickly?

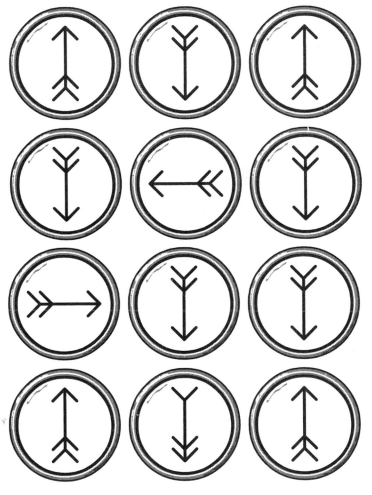

Answer on page 72.

TROUBLING TREE

Can you uncover the pattern in this "tree" and use it to solve for the missing number?

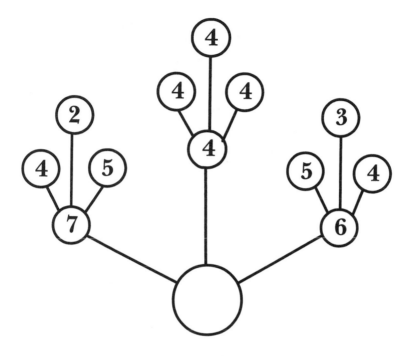

Answer on page 77.

THREE-COLORED CUBE

The cube below has been cut into twenty-seven smaller cubes. These cubes can viewed as three nine-cube slices. So far, so good? Great. Here's where the hard part comes in. Using one of three colors, color each cube. The final colored pattern should have one cube of each color in any three-cube row or three-cube column.

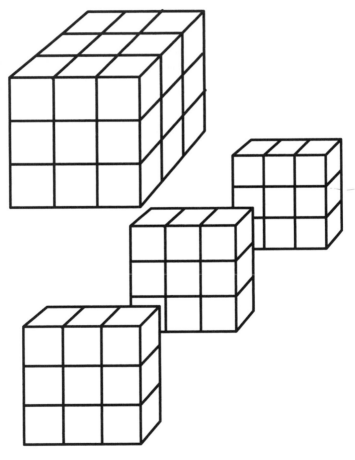

Answer on page 93.

TRYING TRIANGLES

Copy these six patterns onto a sheet of heavy-stock paper. Use a pair of scissors to carefully cut them out. Arrange the shapes into one equal-sided triangle.

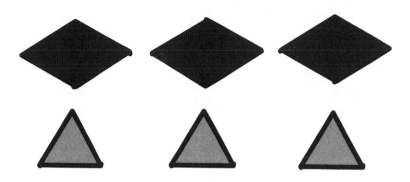

Answer on page 82.

HERE, SPOT

Suppose you could fill in any of the circles of this pattern. How many different and distinguishable patterns could you make?

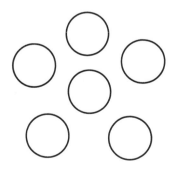

Answer on page 75.

CHALK ONE UP

A large chalk stick has a diameter of an inch. The chalk is packed in a box whose inner space measures 5" × 4". Within this space, twenty pieces of chalk fit snugly. If the box length and width are increased as shown below, the new larger box should hold a maximum of 120 pieces of chalk. Right? Wrong. It can now hold 131 pieces of chalk.

Can you figure out how these extra eleven pieces of chalk fit?

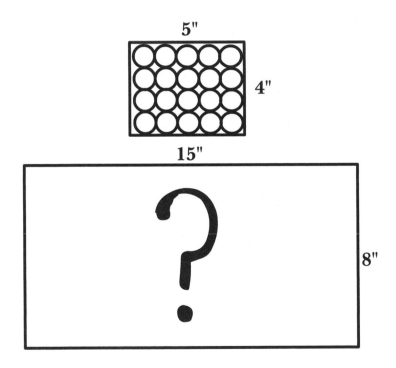

Answer on page 77.

GRID-LOCK

How many different ways can you divide this 4 × 4 grid into two identical parts?

Remember that all of your "dividing lines" must follow along the lines that are all ready in place. Do not count as different ones those that are simply rotations or reflections of others.

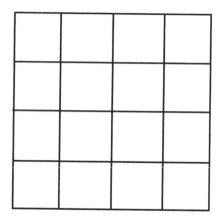

Answer on page 75.

ONLY THE SHADOW KNOWS

Try to imagine a shape that can produce several different shadows. When illuminated from below, it casts a circular shadow. When illuminated from the north, it casts a rectangular shadow. When illuminated from the east, it casts a triangular shadow.

What is the shape of the actual object?

Answer on page 89.

LUCKY ELEVEN?

By connecting different dot sets, you should be able to form eleven different shapes of triangles. Good luck!

FYI: The different triangles include four mirror-image pairs.

Answer on page 77.

STATION SPREAD

Scientists often use visual models to help understand and communicate ideas. Although the following problem is on a global scale, perhaps you can visualize a desktop version of the situation?

Scientists are designing a network of earthquake-monitoring stations. The stations can be built on any surface, but must be located at equal distances from one another. What is the maximum number of stations that can be placed on the Earth and remain equidistant? Oh yes, and where will the stations be placed?

Answer on page 87.

ANSWERS

AMAZE IN STRING
It will come free of the pipe. To visualize this action, start at the pipe. From there, trace the pipe's path out from the center. After a few turns, the pipe exits freely at the opening on the right side of the maze.

BLOCK HEADS
E.

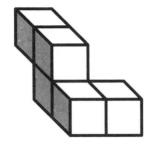

BOXED IN
E cannot be folded into a cube.

BRAIN TRAINING
Six. At every half hour of the journey, you'll pass an incoming train. If you count the inbound train in the Metropolis station and don't count the inbound train in the Gotham City station, you'll pass six trains.

BROKEN RECORD
b) spiral in towards the center spindle (its normal motion). Both sides of the record have an identical spiral. Therefore, if the grooves align, the needle will follow its normal motion towards the center spindle.

CAFFEINE BREAK

4 ounces (about half of pot A). The amount of coffee that can be kept within each pot is determined by the height of the spout opening. The coffee level cannot rise above that spout opening since any extra coffee would spill out from the spout.

CIRCULAR CODE

21. As you move clockwise around the circle, the number on each section is equal to the sum of the two previous sections.

COASTER CUT

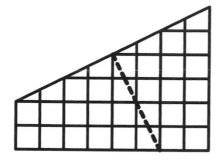

CODE CAPER

CONNECT THE DOTS

Eleven squares.

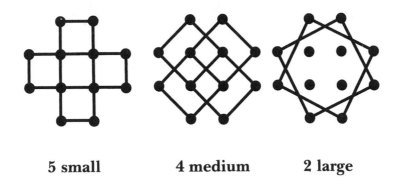

5 small   **4 medium**   **2 large**

CONTROVERSIAL CUBE

Cubes A and D.

DIAL DILEMMA

The dial arrow located in the middle of the bottom row is most unusual. In contrast to the rest, it has two heads and only one tail.

FACES FRONT

Part I: Twenty-two sides.
Part II: Thirty-six sides.

FILL 'ER UP

A	E	G
F	B	I
D	H	C

FOILING FOLDS

FROM WHENCE IT CAME
Pattern D.

GOING IN CIRCLES?

No, the belts are arranged in a pattern that doesn't allow them to move.

GOING TO PIECES

Four colors. It doesn't matter how many common borders there are. The maximum number of colors needed to distinguish any number of adjoining pieces will always be four.

HANDS-ON/MINDS-OFF

The bottom-row center hand is unlike the others. It alone is a right hand.

HIDDEN IN PLANE SITE

The fifteen squares are:
one 4 × 4 square;
two 3 × 3 squares;
four 2 × 2 squares;
eight 1 × 1 square.

IMAGING DIGITS

The digit 1 appears 21 times. The digit 0 appears only 11 times.

IMPOSSIBLE PROFILE

C.

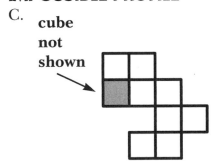

cube
not
shown

GRID-LOCK

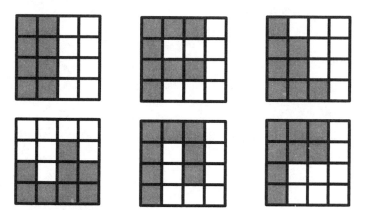

HERE, SPOT
Sixteen distinguishable patterns.

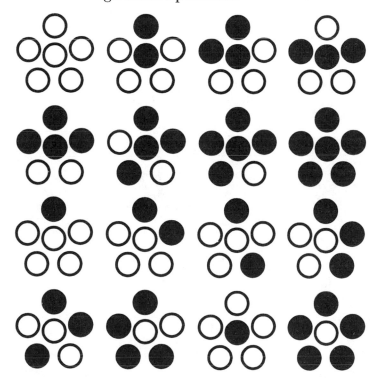

INTO THE POOL
Two solutions are shown.

⑤   ②   ①   ③

① ④ ⑦   or   ⑥ ④ ②

⑥   ③   ⑤   ⑦

LET THE GAMES BEGIN
B. Here's why:

CHALK ONE UP

It all depends upon how you pack the chalk. In straight rows and columns, only 120 pieces can fit. However, if the chalk pieces are staggered so they fill up some of the waste space, 131 pieces can fit.

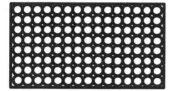 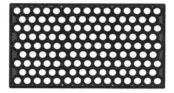

Lucky Eleven

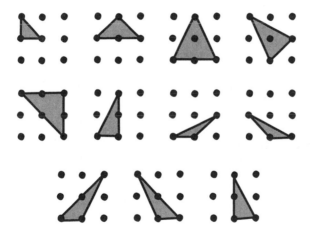

Trouble Tree

9. The numbers are obtained by adding together the values of the two circles that are attached by diagonal lines. Then the value within the circle directly atop is subtracted from this sum. In the final grouping, it's 7 + 6 − 9, or 9.

LINK LATCH

Just open the bottom link. The top two links are not attached to each other.

MIRROR MADNESS

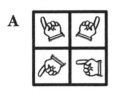

MORE OF THE GREAT DIVIDE

MORE SPOTS

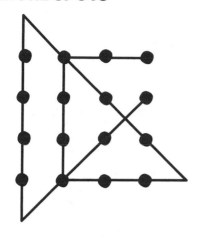

NAUGHTY NOTES

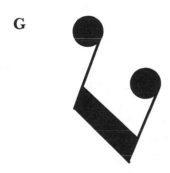

G is a mirror image of the other note pairs. All other pairs can be made by rotating another pair.

NESTING DOLLS

The final height of the stack approaches 2 feet. Although there are an infinite number of dolls, the size of each doll diminishes. Mathematically that works out to 1 ft. + ½ ft. + ¼ ft. + 1/8 ft. + 1/16 ft. + 1/32 ft. ...

ON THE MARCH

Part I   Part II

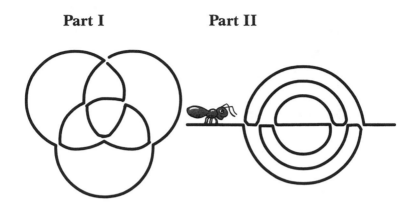

OUT OF THIS WORLD CONSTRUCTION

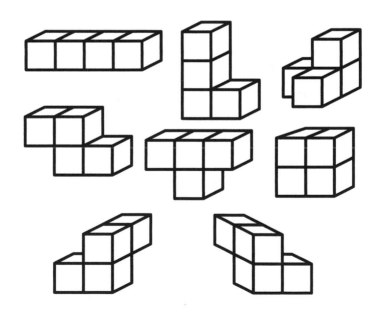

PENCIL STACK
Pencil #7

PENTAGON PIECES

PHARAOH FOLDS
B is the only pattern that will produce a four-sided triangular pyramid.

PI PIECES

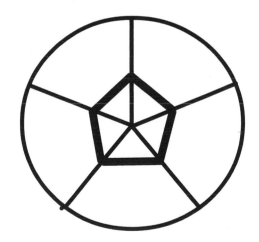

PIZZA PI PROBLEM

Seven sections:

POINT THE WAY

D. Each tile is rotated from the pervious one by ¼ turn.

PREFAB 4

C

TRYING TRIANGLES

PUZZLING PAGES

56 pages. Here's how the numbers are arranged on each double sheet.

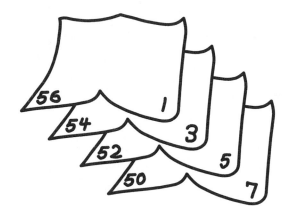

RACK EM, AGAIN, AGAIN, AND AGAIN

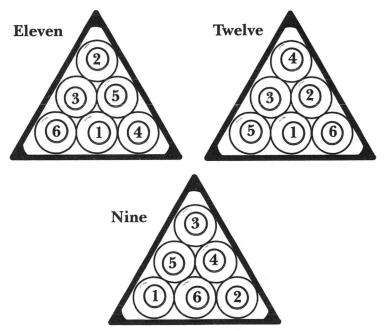

Eleven

Twelve

Nine

REFLECTING BACK
Part I

Part II

ROLL WITH IT
D.

SHAKES
Fifteen handshakes. The first person would have shaken hands five times. The next person only needed to make four handshakes, since the handshake with one person had all ready been completed. The next person required only three, and so on. That gives us $5+4+3+2+1 = 15$.

SINK YOUR TEETH
Since they have the same number of teeth, they will spin at the same speed. Cog C does not affect the rate of teeth passage; it only transfers the passage of teeth from cog B to cog D.

SECTOR SEVER

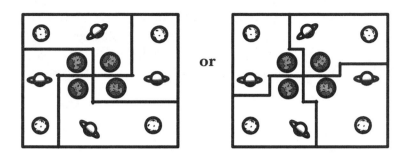

or

SIZING UP SQUARES

Five sizes:

Twenty squares.

SNEAKY

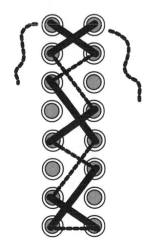

SPACING OUT

No. To best visualize her path, let's undo the cube into its component flattened faces. From this diagram, you can see that the shortest distance between two points is a straight line. That line does not coincide with her planned path (shown as a dotted line).

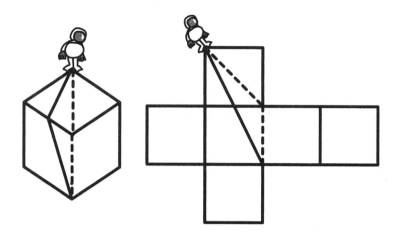

SPIRAL BOUND

Block F. All five other blocks are identical. Block F is a mirror image of these blocks.

SPOTTY ANSWERS

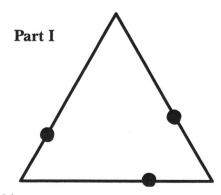

Part I

Part II

SQUARE DEAL

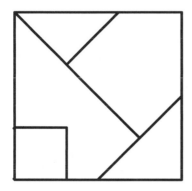

STATION SPREAD

Four stations. Each station is placed at the corner of a four-sided pyramid (tetrahedron) that is inscribed within the planet.

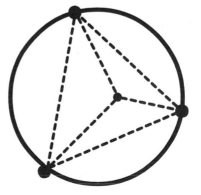

SQUARE GEARS

The bottom gear would continue to spin as if both gears were circular.

STOP AND THINK

Eighteen, but you don't have to trace out each one. The easiest way to solve this puzzle is to start at the beginning and determine the number of paths that can get you to an intersection. The number of paths to each successive intersection is equal to the sum of the paths that are "attached" to it.

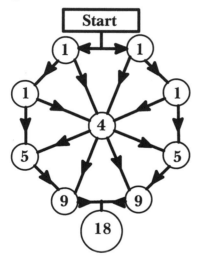

SUPERIMPOSING POSITION

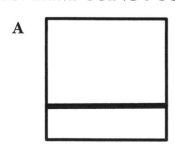

A

SURE SHOT

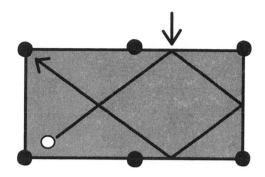

ONLY THE SHADOW KNOWS

It is a cylinder that has been cut into a wedge. Two slices that extend from the upper diameter to opposite sides of the bottom have been removed to form this shape.

THE CIRCLE GAME

27. The number at the center of any circle is equal to the sum of the number located on its outline.

THE JIG'S UP

Forty-nine moves. The sequence and strategy in which the pieces are assembled will not affect the number of moves. Fifty pieces require forty-nine independent joining "events".

THE WHOLE TRUTH

Cut out an L-shaped section and rotate it to the opposite corner of the piece with the hole.

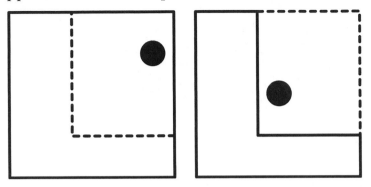

THIS SIDE UP

The extra figure is "formed" within the center of this pattern.

TOOTHPICK TRICKS

Part I

Part II

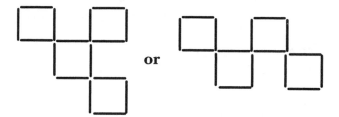

or their reflections

Part III

Part IV

HOW MANY TRIANGLES?

27 triangles: 16 one-cell triangles, 7 four-cell triangles, 3 nine-cell triangles, and 1 sixteen-cell triangle.

TYING THE KNOT

A knot *will* form in the spaghetti.

VERY WELL VENN

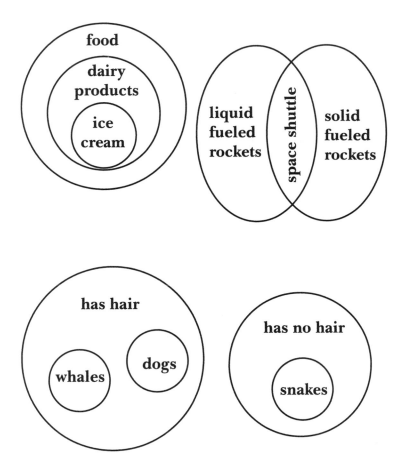

THREE-COLORED CUBE

THIS WHEEL'S ON FIRE
In the top set, the large wheel will spin the exact same way as the smaller wheel. In the bottom set, the top wheel will first move clockwise. Then, before completing a rotation, it will reverse direction.

WHAT'S NEXT?
10. The sequence is formed by first doubling a number and then subtracting one from the product.

WHAT SIGN ARE YOU?

$$5 \boxtimes 2 \boxminus 3 \boxplus 5 \boxdiv 4 = 3$$

WRAP IT UP

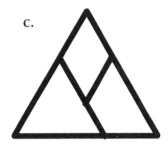

c.

CUT THE CUBE

The cut must bisect the cube in half as shown below. The exposed inner surface is flat and has the shape of a hexagon.

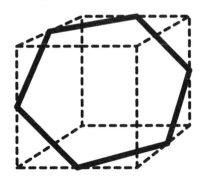

Index

About the Author

Michael DiSpezio has always had a fondness for integrating learning with creativity, critical thinking, and performance. After tiring of "counting hairs on copepods," Michael traded the marine science laboratory for the classroom. Over the years, he has taught physics, chemistry, mathematics, and rock 'n' roll musical theater. During his classroom years, Michael co-authored a chemistry book, which launched his writing career.

To date, Michael is the author of *Critical Thinking Puzzles*, *Great Critical Thinking Puzzles*, and *Challenging Critical Thinking Puzzles* (all from Sterling) as well as eighteen science textbooks, a producer of several educational videos, and a creator of hundreds of supplementary products and science education articles. His most recent science education project was authoring *The Science of HIV*, a teaching package published by the National Association of Science Teachers.

Michael's expertise in both video and science education has resulted in several trips to train counterparts in the Middle East. When he isn't presenting workshops for science teachers, Michael is at home writing, creating, and puzzle solving.